We Believe
LEADER GUIDE

**We Believe:
How the Nicene Creed
Can Deepen Your Faith**

We Believe
978-1-7910-3560-0
978-1-7910-3561-7 *eBook*

We Believe: DVD
978-1-7910-3564-8

We Believe: Leader Guide
978-1-7910-3562-4
978-1-7910-3563-1 *eBook*

We Believe

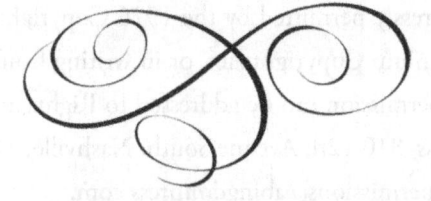

How the Nicene Creed Can Deepen Your Faith

LEADER GUIDE

Michael Carpenter

Abingdon Press | Nashville

We Believe
How the Nicene Creed Can Deepen Your Faith
Leader Guide

Copyright © 2025 Abingdon Press
All rights reserved.

No part of this work may be reproduced or transmitted in any form or by any means, electronic or mechanical, including photocopying and recording, or by any information storage or retrieval system, except as may be expressly permitted by the 1976 Copyright Act, the 1998 Digital Millennium Copyright Act, or in writing from the publisher. Requests for permission can be addressed to Rights and Permissions, Abingdon Press, 810 12th Avenue South, Nashville, TN 37203-4704 or emailed to permissions@abingdonpress.com.

978-1-7910-3562-4

Scripture quotations unless noted otherwise are taken from the New Revised Standard Version, Updated Edition. Copyright © 2021 National Council of Churches of Christ in the United States of America. Used by permission. All rights reserved worldwide.

MANUFACTURED IN THE UNITED STATES OF AMERICA

CONTENTS

Introduction 7

Session 1: We Believe in One God 10

Session 2: Of One Being with the Father 18

Session 3: For Us and for Our Salvation 27

Session 4: In Accordance with the Scriptures. 36

Session 5: With the Father and the Son. 45

Session 6: One, Holy, Catholic, and Apostolic 53

About the Leader Guide Writer

The Rev. Michael S. Poteet is an ordained Minister of Word and Sacrament in the Presbyterian Church (U.S.A.). A graduate of the College of William and Mary and Princeton Theological Seminary, he serves the larger church as a Christian education writer, biblical storyteller, and guest preacher. You can find his occasional musings on the meetings of faith and fiction at http://www.bibliomike.com.

INTRODUCTION

In *We Believe: How the Nicene Creed Can Deepen Your Faith*, the Rev. Michael Carpenter (lead pastor, Lost Creek United Methodist Church in Stillwater, Oklahoma) invites readers to become more familiar with, or to consider seriously for the first time, the Nicene Creed—an early fourth-century summary of the Christian faith that is one of the great ecumenical creeds still used in the worldwide Church today. Michael hopes readers will discover, as he has, how the creed can strengthen what they already believe, spur them to new depths of belief, and help them rediscover and build upon the "bedrock" of their faith.

This Leader Guide is intended to help you lead a small group of adults from your congregation in your own study of the Nicene Creed, using Scripture and Michael's book as your primary resources. Here you will find logistical pointers, Scripture readings, and study questions you can use to plan and lead six sessions, corresponding to the six chapters of Michael's book:

- Session 1: We Believe in One God introduces participants to the creed and its history and highlights its continuity with Jewish and Christian belief in one God. It also asks how this belief continues to challenge idolatry in culture and church today.

Introduction

- Session 2: Of One Being with the Father explores the creed's teaching about the relationship between God the Father and God the Son. It also asks what difference professing Jesus Christ as "Lord" makes today.
- Session 3: For Us and for Our Salvation examines the creed's teaching about the Incarnation. It also challenges participants to consider how they might "incarnate" God's Word in their circumstances.
- Session 4: In Accordance with the Scriptures invites participants to see why and how the creed finds the Old Testament anticipating Jesus's ministry, especially his death and resurrection. It also invites reflection on the continuing importance of Jesus's ascension and his promised return in judgment.
- Session 5: With the Father and the Son considers some biblical foundations for the creed's teaching about the Holy Spirit. It also asks participants to identify specific ways they can follow and participate in the Spirit's life-giving mission.
- Session 6: One, Holy, Catholic, and Apostolic examines the creed's four marks of the Church in the light of several New Testament Scriptures about the Church. It also encourages participants' ongoing engagement with the creed.

Although this Leader Guide is written with the assumption that both leaders and participants will also be reading *We Believe*, its quotations from Michael's book and its direct references to Scripture mean it can also be used on its own.

Each session contains the following elements to draw from as you plan six in-person, virtual, or hybrid sessions:

- Session Goals
- Biblical Foundations—Scripture texts for the session, in the New Revised Standard Version Updated Edition;

Introduction

- Before Your Session—Tips to help you prepare a productive session.
- Starting Your Session—Discussion questions intended to warm up your group for fruitful discussion;
- Opening Prayer—Use the prayer as written or let it suggest a prayer in your own words;
- Book Discussion Questions—You likely will not be able or want to use all the questions in every session, so feel free to pick and choose based on your group's interests and the Spirit's leading;
- Closing Your Session—A focused discussion or reflection, often suggesting action to take beyond the session; and
- Closing Prayer—Each session suggests a hymn or spiritual for use as a closing prayer, highlighting how the songs a congregation sings also, over time, can become a kind of informal "creed."

Thank you for your willingness to lead! May you and your group find your study of this ancient treasure of the Christian faith interesting and invigorating, and may it inspire you to a fuller and more fulfilling faith in the triune God to whom the Nicene Creed witnesses!

SESSION 1

We Believe in One God

Session Goals

This season's reading, discussion, and prayer will help participants:

- reflect on their personal and congregational engagement with creeds in general and the Nicene Creed in particular, appreciating the Church's intent in developing creeds;
- understand basic facts about the formulation and nature of the Nicene Creed;
- appreciate the importance of the Shema in Jewish belief, including Jesus's belief;
- articulate and consider the significance of the Nicene Creed's affirmations about God the Father; and
- evaluate Paul's speech in Athens (Acts 17:22-34) as an attempt to communicate the gospel in a culture full of idols, recognizing parallels to society today.

We Believe in One God

Biblical Foundations

*Hear, O Israel: The L*ORD *is our God, the L*ORD *alone. You shall love the L*ORD *your God with all your heart and with all your soul and with all your might. Keep these words that I am commanding you today in your heart. Recite them to your children and talk about them when you are at home and when you are away, when you lie down and when you rise. Bind them as a sign on your hand, fix them as an emblem on your forehead, and write them on the doorposts of your house and on your gates.*

Deuteronomy 6:4-9

Then Paul stood in front of the Areopagus and said, "Athenians, I see how extremely spiritual you are in every way. For as I went through the city and looked carefully at the objects of your worship, I found among them an altar with the inscription, 'To an unknown god.' What therefore you worship as unknown, this I proclaim to you. The God who made the world and everything in it, he who is Lord of heaven and earth, does not live in shrines made by human hands, nor is he served by human hands, as though he needed anything, since he himself gives to all mortals life and breath and all things. From one ancestor he made all peoples to inhabit the whole earth, and he allotted the times of their existence and the boundaries of the places where they would live, so that they would search for God and perhaps fumble about for him and find him—though indeed he is not far from each one of us. For 'In him we live and move and have our being'; as even some of your own poets have said,

'For we, too, are his offspring.'"

Acts 17:22-28

Before Your Session

- Carefully and prayerfully read this session's Biblical Foundations, more than once. Note words and phrases that attract your attention, and meditate on them. Make special note of how these Gospel stories are the same and different.

- Write down questions you have, and try to answer them, consulting trusted Bible commentaries.
- Carefully read the introduction and chapter 1 of *We Believe*, more than once.
- You will need either Bibles for in-person participants or screen slides prepared with Scripture texts for sharing (identify the translation used), or both; newsprint or a markerboard and markers (for in-person sessions); paper, pens or pencils (in-person).
- If using the DVD or streaming video, preview the Session 1 video segment. Choose the best time in your session plan for viewing it.
- Put the text of the Nicene Creed (in the translation your denomination or congregation uses, if applicable) either on a paper handout, a slide for screen sharing, or both.

Starting Your Session

Welcome participants. Briefly explain why you are excited to lead this study of *We Believe* by Michael Carpenter. Invite volunteers to talk briefly about what they want to gain from this study.

Tell participants a "creed" is a formal statement of beliefs. In *We Believe*, Michael compares a creed to an "elevator pitch"—a brief summary of the most important points about a subject, designed to quickly communicate what it is and why it matters.

Distribute or display the text of the Nicene Creed. Invite participants to read it aloud with you in unison. Discuss:

- On a scale of 1 to 5 with 1 representing "I've never seen it before" and 5 representing "I could recite it in my sleep," how familiar are you with the Nicene Creed?
- What word or phrase in the Nicene Creed most grabs your attention, and why?
- What questions, if any, does the Nicene Creed leave you asking?

We Believe in One God

- If you are familiar with the Apostles' Creed, how is the Nicene Creed like and unlike it? What do you think about these differences?
- How important are the Nicene Creed or other creeds in your congregation's worship, and why?
- How much do you, personally, value creeds, and why?

Opening Prayer

Holy God, we praise you for creating and claiming a holy people for yourself. You liberated the children of Abraham and Sarah from their slavery in Egypt, freeing them to worship and serve you alone; and through your Son Jesus, you joined us to your royal priesthood, that we, too, may proclaim your mighty acts. We thank you for the faithful who have gone before us, leaving a legacy of faith to instruct and encourage us. May the same Spirit who guided the Church as it declared the Nicene Creed guide your Church today, that your blessing may flow through Christ's family to all families. Amen.

[Read aloud]

Watch Session Video

Watch the Session 1 video segment together. Discuss:

- Which of Michael's statements most interested, intrigued, surprised, or confused you? Why?
- What questions does this video segment raise for you?

The Nicene Nitty-Gritty

Ask any participants who have ever attended a meeting of a larger church body (for example, districts, conferences, synods, presbyteries, ecumenical gatherings) to briefly describe the experience. What were the most important matters on the agenda? Who got to speak? How were decisions made? Would you want to attend again? Why or why not? (*Optional:* If you know ahead of time no one in your group has attended such a meeting, either invite a church member or pastor who

We Believe: Leader Guide

has, contact your local governing body, if any, for resources to share that interpret its nature and mission, or both.)

Tell participants the Nicene Creed is the product of an ancient meeting of the larger Church. In a conversational mini-lecture, present these basic facts from *We Believe*:

- When, in the early 300s, Emperor Constantine converted to Christianity and legalized it in the Roman Empire, he convened an ecumenical (churchwide) gathering of leaders to settle controversial questions of doctrine (official church teaching).
- The council met in Nicaea—less than one hundred miles from Constantine's capital of Constantinople, in what is today Iznik, Turkey—beginning in May 325.
- The 318 bishops who attended the council brought entourages of secretaries and staff, bringing total attendance to likely more than two thousand people. Constantine himself also attended.
- In addition to producing the Nicene Creed, the council appointed bishops, discussed church discipline, and settled the date for celebrating Easter.
- Strictly speaking, the creed we are studying is a version expanded at the Council of Constantinople in 381 (the Niceno-Constantinopolitan Creed), but the majority of the Church calls it "the Nicene Creed" for simplicity's sake.

Discuss:

- What personal and political factors may have motivated Constantine to seek a church united in its doctrine? Is unity of doctrine a realistic and desirable goal today? Why or why not?
- When, if ever, have you discussed differences and "the common core" of faith with other Christians, as Michael did with his college fraternity brothers? How, if at all, have these conversations influenced your faith?

- How important is it for Christians to seek out conversations and relationships with those of different beliefs on an ongoing basis? Why?
- Why did C. S. Lewis compare the Nicene Creed to a map? Does his analogy help you better understand the nature and intent of the Nicene Creed? Why or why not?

One God

Point out that the Nicene Creed (like the Apostles' Creed and many other creeds) is organized in a trinitarian format, with sections focused on each person of the Trinity (Father, Son, and Holy Spirit).

Recruit a volunteer to read aloud Deuteronomy 6:4-9. Tell participants verse 4 is known as the Shema in Judaism, after its first word in Hebrew, and is an "essential declaration" about God. Discuss:

- What claim does the Shema make about "the Lord" (YHWH), the God of Israel?
- Verse 4 can be read as saying "the Lord alone" or "the Lord is one." How, if at all, do you think these two statements differ?
- What is Israel commanded to do in response to the Shema's claim about God?
- Read Mark 12:28-34. What did Jesus teach about the Shema?
- What concrete, practical forms does loving God with our whole heart, soul, and might take?

Our Father, the Almighty, the Maker

Recruit a volunteer to read aloud Acts 17:22-28 (29-34). Discuss:

- Why was the Church's belief in one God "scandalous and offensive" in the ancient Roman world, as Michael states and as Acts 17 illustrates?

- Why does the biblical faith in one God exclude the possibility of worshiping other gods?
- How does Paul present his faith in the Athenians' "extremely spiritual" (v. 22) context?
- Paul claims even the Athenians know they are God's "offspring" (vv. 28-29). Why does Scripture often picture God as "Father" (for example: Hosea 11:1-4; Psalm 103:13; Matthew 6:31-33)? How well do you think Paul expresses the "familial and relational qualities" Michael says calling God "Father" is meant to express?
- Michael writes that, just as a human father relates to each of his children differently, God's fatherhood "is unique to each of us." Do you think of or experience God as Father? Why or why not?
- Do you think other names or images say what "Father" means to say about God? If so, which ones? If not, why not?
- Michael says calling God "Father Almighty" communicates both the closeness (immanence) and the power and authority (the transcendence) of God. Generally, at which end of this spectrum are most of your ideas about and experiences of God? Why is it important "to hold tightly to both God's immanence and transcendence," as Michael says the Nicene Creed does?
- What argument does Paul make against the Athenians' religious practices (vv. 29-31)?
- "When we view idolatry not as simply worshiping an idol but instead as giving our ultimate allegiance to something other than God and finding our value in it, some common idols come into view." How do you see idols tempting people today, in the culture and in the Church?
- How does Michael distinguish between the way humans create and the way God creates? How does this distinction help guard against idolatry? When has a human material or artistic creation helped you glorify the Creator of all?

- How effectively do you think Paul's speech in Athens communicates the gospel in a culture full of idols, and why? How can Paul's experience inform and encourage us in our efforts to communicate the gospel in society today?

Closing Your Session

Read aloud from *We Believe*: "God is not just the Almighty; God is the Almighty Father.... When it comes to the problems and trials of life, you are not alone. In your corner is your Almighty Father, whose 'power at work within us is able to accomplish abundantly far more than all we can ask or imagine' (Ephesians 3:20). That's how big your God is."

Invite participants to think about a problem they or someone for whom they care is facing. Ask those who wish to do so to briefly talk about the problem so your entire group can pray for the situation. Encourage participants to keep these problems in mind during the Closing Prayer.

Closing Prayer

For your closing prayer, sing together or read this verse from "Praise to the Lord, the Almighty" (Joachim Neander, 1680; trans., Catherine Winkworth, 1863; https://hymnary.org/text/praise_to_the_lord_the_almighty_the_king) or another hymn or song you think relates to the subjects of this session.

Praise to the Lord, the Almighty, the King of creation!
O my soul, praise him, for he is your health and salvation!
Come, all who hear; now to his temple draw near,
join me in glad adoration.

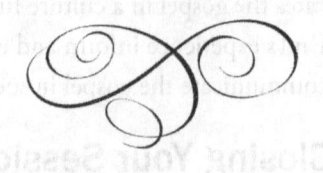

SESSION 2
Of One Being with the Father

Session Goals

This season's reading, discussion, and prayer will help participants:

- understand how and why the teaching of Arius occasioned the Council of Nicaea;
- reflect on what the controversy over Arianism can teach the Church today about heresy;
- Consider what it meant for early Christians to profess Jesus as Messiah (Christ) and Lord and what these same claims mean for them and their congregations today;
- Identify claims about Jesus's relationship to God in Philippians 2 and Hebrews 1, relating them to the teaching of the Nicene Creed; and
- articulate why Jesus's full divinity matters to their faith.

Biblical Foundations

When John heard in prison what the Messiah was doing, he sent word by his disciples and said to him, "Are you the one who is to come, or are we to wait for another?" Jesus answered them, "Go and tell John what you hear and see: the blind receive their sight, the lame walk, those with a skin disease are cleansed, the deaf hear, the dead are raised, and the poor have good news brought to them. And blessed is anyone who takes no offense at me."

Matthew 11:2-6

Let the same mind be in you that was in Christ Jesus,

> *who, though he existed in the form of God,*
> > *did not regard equality with God*
> > *as something to be grasped,*
>
> *but emptied himself,*
> > *taking the form of a slave,*
> > *assuming human likeness.*
>
> *And being found in appearance as a human,*
> > *he humbled himself*
> > *and became obedient to the point of death—*
> > *even death on a cross.*
>
> *Therefore God exalted him even more highly*
> > *and gave him the name*
> > *that is above every other name,*
>
> *so that at the name given to Jesus*
> > *every knee should bend,*
> > *in heaven and on earth and under the earth,*
>
> *and every tongue should confess*
> > *that Jesus Christ is Lord,*
> > *to the glory of God the Father.*

Philippians 2:5-11

Long ago God spoke to our ancestors in many and various ways by the prophets, but in these last days he has spoken to us by a Son, whom he appointed heir of all things, through whom he also created the worlds. He is the reflection of God's glory and the exact imprint of God's very being, and he sustains all things by his powerful word. When he had made purification for sins, he sat down at the right hand of the Majesty on high, having become as much superior to angels as the name he has inherited is more excellent than theirs.

We Believe: Leader Guide

For to which of the angels did God ever say,

> *"You are my Son;*
> *today I have begotten you"?*

Or again,

> *"I will be his Father,*
> *and he will be my Son"?*
>
> *Hebrews 1:1-5*

Before Your Session

- Carefully and prayerfully read this session's Biblical Foundations, more than once. Note words and phrases that attract your attention, and meditate on them. Make special note of how these Gospel stories are the same and different. Write down questions you have, and try to answer them, consulting trusted Bible commentaries.
- Carefully read chapter 2 of *We Believe*, more than once.
- You will need either Bibles for in-person participants or screen slides prepared with Scripture texts for sharing (identify the translation used), or both; newsprint or a markerboard and markers (for in-person sessions); paper, pens or pencils (in-person).
- If using the DVD or streaming video, preview the Session 2 video segment. Choose the best time in your session plan for viewing it.
- Put the text of the Nicene Creed (in the translation your denomination or congregation uses, if applicable) either on a paper handout, a slide for screen sharing, or both.

Starting Your Session

Welcome participants. Ask volunteers to recall and recite some of the catchiest advertising slogans they can. Discuss:

- Why do marketers so often rely on slogans?
- What are the hallmarks of a "good slogan"?
- If you were to adopt a slogan for yourself or for your congregation, what would it be?

Note that Michael writes in *We Believe* that "everyone loves a good slogan. And...people will even love a bad slogan." Tell participants that, in this session, your group will explore the way the Nicene Creed refutes a popular slogan about Jesus from the early fourth century.

Distribute or display the text of the Nicene Creed. Invite participants to read it aloud, either in its entirety or from "We believe in one Lord" through "all things were made." Read aloud from *We Believe*: "What the Nicene Creed says about Jesus can unlock for us a greater love of our Savior and a richer life of faith."

Opening Prayer

Eternal and Sovereign God, who dwells in unapproachable light and whom none have seen or can see: We praise you for graciously choosing to reveal yourself in your Son, Jesus Christ. May your Spirit guide us as we seek greater understanding of how you have spoken in your Word made flesh, that we may echo your loving will in all we say and do. Amen.

Watch Session Video

Watch the Session 2 video segment together. Discuss:

- Which of Michael's statements most interested, intrigued, surprised, or confused you? Why?
- What questions does this video segment raise for you?

The Catchy Slogan That Caused a Council

In a conversational mini-lecture, share with participants these facts from *We Believe* about Arius:

- Arius was a fourth-century priest in Alexandria, Egypt—"a devoted and sincere man of faith who took very seriously the core tenets of Christianity."
- In his concern to honor biblical witness to both the oneness of God and Jesus's special relationship to God, Arius taught "Jesus is indeed divine, but not in the same way as God the Father.... Arius claimed the Son had to come later than the Father and was subordinate to him."
- Arius used the slogan "There was when he was not," referring to the Son, to summarize and spread his teaching.
- Arius's bishop, Alexander, denounced Arius's teaching; however, at one point in the 320s, a third of priests under Alexander supported Arius against the bishop.
- The question of how to properly understand the Son's nature and relationship to the Father was the main issue before the Council of Nicaea.
- The council taught that the Son is "eternally begotten of the Father"—"outside of time," "before all ages"—meaning, against Arius's slogan, there was *no* time when the Son was not.
- The council rejected the compromise position that the Son is "of a similar nature" (Greek, *homoiousios*) to the Father and taught the Son is "of the same nature" or "of one being with the Father" (*homoousios*).
- Although he was "a faithful man trying to make the faith understandable for those in his flock," Arius is remembered as a heretic for his doctrinally incorrect teaching.

Discuss:

- Why was Arius's teaching about the Son controversial?
- What theological or practical difference(s) does it make whether the Son is divine in the same way as the Father?

- Have you ever wondered how to reconcile Scripture's claims about the oneness of God and the divinity of Jesus? If not, why not? If so, what have you found helpful in thinking about this issue?
- Arius taught Jesus was the divine Son yet subordinate to God. Where and how, if at all, is "Arianism" still present in church and culture today?
- Should the Church today still concern itself with refuting theological heresy—especially if, as Michael states, "heretics" don't hold to "false beliefs so they [can] hurt the Church"? If not, why not? If so, how?
- How can we distinguish today between "heresies" and honestly held but equally faithful differences in belief or opinion?

Jesus, Messiah and Lord

Read aloud from *We Believe*: "At the Council of Nicaea, the preeminent leaders of the Church in 325 arrived at a new level of clarity about God the Son.... But to make that clarification, they [had to use] a word not found anywhere in Scripture." Tell participants, as Michael does, that the Church was developing the Nicene Creed at the same time that the canon of the New Testament was developing and that Christians believe the same Holy Spirit inspired both processes. For the rest of this session, your group will consider Scripture passages related to the ideas expressed in the Nicene Creed about Jesus.

Recruit a volunteer to read aloud Matthew 11:2-6. Discuss:

- Why does John, who earlier in Matthew treated Jesus as his superior (3:13-15), now question whether Jesus is "the one who is to come" (v. 3)?
- How does Jesus respond to John's question (vv. 4-6)? How satisfactory do you imagine John found Jesus's answer? How satisfactory do you find it? Why?

- Michael says the Messiah, or "Anointed One," was expected to be "the one who would fulfill all God's promises." The Greek word for "Messiah" is *Christ*. Why did and do Jesus's followers call him Messiah, or Christ?
- Michael points out that kings, priests, and prophets in the Old Testament were also "anointed ones" (e.g., 1 Samuel 16:13; Exodus 30:22-33). How might each of these types of "messiahs" help us understand why Jesus's followers call him Christ?
- From earliest times, Jesus's followers also called him "Lord." Why did devout first-century Jews, who professed faith in the God of Israel as "the Lord alone" (Deuteronomy 6:4), call Jesus "Lord"? What do Christians today mean—and what do *you* mean—in calling Jesus "Lord"? How is Jesus like and unlike other actual or would-be "lords"?
- Under the Roman Empire before Constantine, the claim "Jesus is Lord" was subversive and countercultural because society proclaimed Caesar as Lord. Michael states "the declaration 'Jesus is Lord, so Caesar is not' still reorients us." How does your and your congregation's profession of Jesus as Lord challenge claims of lordship that politicians and government officials may make? How does your faith inform your politics, as Michael states it should?
- Michael says the profession "Jesus is Lord" also means "I am not." When and how do you and your congregation struggle to submit yourselves to Jesus's authority?

Two Scriptures About Jesus's Relationship to God

Form two groups of participants. Assign one group to read and discuss Philippians 2:5-11, and the other, Hebrews 1:1-5. Instruct each group to pay special attention in their discussion to what the assigned Scripture says about the relationship between God and Jesus. After allowing sufficient time for discussion, bring all participants back together and invite a volunteer from each of the two groups to talk briefly about highlights of the discussion.

Discuss the two Scriptures further:

- What does Paul, or the early Christian hymn he may here be quoting, say about Jesus's relationship to God? How, if at all, did this relationship change over the course of Jesus's obedience? How, if at all, will it change in the future?
- What does Hebrews 1 say about Jesus's relationship to God?
- Do the passages from Philippians and Hebrews agree in any way about Jesus and his relationship with God? Do they disagree? If so, how?
- What do we know from each of these Scriptures about Jesus's divinity? His humanity? His existence from and involvement in creation? His death and resurrection? His lordship and authority?
- Do either of these Scriptures, taken by themselves, leave room for Arius's teaching about Jesus? Why or why not?
- How much or how little do you think the Nicene Creed's affirmations about Jesus align with what these Scriptures tell us about Jesus?
- What other Scriptures can you think of or find that could help us better understand Jesus's relationship to God?

Closing Your Session

Read aloud from *We Believe*: "If Jesus were not fully God, then what was accomplished in his life, death, and resurrection? If Jesus is only partially God, then we are only partially saved, partially restored, partially reborn. But we are not partially saved. We are fully saved, fully restored, fully reborn, because Jesus our Lord and Savior is also fully God."

Discuss:

- How important do you feel Jesus's full divinity is to your faith?
- How would you respond to someone who questions whether Jesus has fully saved because we continue to see and experience sin, evil, and death in our world and in our lives?
- Michael writes that our "full salvation is accomplished not by our own efforts, but in surrendering those efforts to the Son of God who has already accomplished it for us." What efforts do both you and your congregation need to surrender to Jesus in this confidence?

Closing Prayer

For your closing prayer, sing together or read this verse of the Christmas hymn "O Come, All Ye Faithful" (attr. John Francis Wade; trans. Frederick Oakley, 1841; https://hymnary.org/text/o_come_all_ye_faithful_joyful_and_triump); or another hymn or song you think relates to the subjects of this session.

God of God, Light of Light,
lo, He abhors not the virgin's womb;
very God, begotten not created;
O come, let us adore Him;
O come, let us adore Him;
O come, let us adore Him, Christ, the Lord!

SESSION 3

For Us and for Our Salvation

Session Goals

This season's reading, discussion, and prayer will help participants:

- understand why the Nicene Creed's discussion of Jesus's life focuses on the Incarnation and the Crucifixion and Resurrection, without mention of the rest of his life;
- define the heresy of Docetism and appreciate why the Council of Nicaea rejected it;
- explore the doctrine of the Incarnation by reading, comparing, and contrasting John 1:1-18 and Luke 1:26-38.
- appreciate the "scandal of particularity" in Luke's account of Jesus's birth;
- ponder the redemptive nature of Jesus's suffering and death; and
- identify ways in which to continue the "incarnating" of Christ in the world today.

Biblical Foundations

In the beginning was the Word, and the Word was with God, and the Word was God. He was in the beginning with God. All things came into being through him, and without him not one thing came into being. What has come into being in him was life, and the life was the light of all people. The light shines in the darkness, and the darkness did not overtake it.... And the Word became flesh and lived among us, and we have seen his glory, the glory as of a father's only son, full of grace and truth.

John 1:1-5, 14

Mary said to the angel, "How can this be, since I am a virgin?" The angel said to her, "The Holy Spirit will come upon you, and the power of the Most High will overshadow you; therefore the child to be born will be holy; he will be called Son of God.

Luke 1:34-35

In those days a decree went out from Caesar Augustus that all the world should be registered. This was the first registration and was taken while Quirinius was governor of Syria. All went to their own towns to be registered. Joseph also went from the town of Nazareth in Galilee to Judea, to the city of David called Bethlehem, because he was descended from the house and family of David. He went to be registered with Mary, to whom he was engaged and who was expecting a child.

Luke 2:1-5

Surely he has borne our infirmities
*   and carried our diseases,*
yet we accounted him stricken,
*   struck down by God, and afflicted.*
But he was wounded for our transgressions,
*   crushed for our iniquities;*
upon him was the punishment that made us whole,
*   and by his bruises we are healed.*
All we like sheep have gone astray;
*   we have all turned to our own way,*

and the LORD *has laid on him*
   the iniquity of us all.
                                    Isaiah 53:4-6

Before Your Session

- Carefully and prayerfully read this session's Biblical Foundations, more than once. Note words and phrases that attract your attention, and meditate on them. Make special note of how these Gospel stories are the same and different. Write down questions you have, and try to answer them, consulting trusted Bible commentaries.
- Carefully read chapter 3 of *We Believe*, more than once.
- You will need either Bibles for in-person participants or screen slides prepared with Scripture texts for sharing (identify the translation used), or both; newsprint or a markerboard and markers (for in-person sessions); paper, pens or pencils (in-person).
- If using the DVD or streaming video, preview the Session 3 video segment. Choose the best time in your session plan for viewing it.
- Put the text of the Nicene Creed (in the translation your denomination or congregation uses, if applicable) either on a paper handout, a slide for screen sharing, or both.

Starting Your Session

Welcome participants. Ask participants to name everything they can think of about Jesus's life *other than* anything associated exclusively with Christmas, Good Friday, or Easter. Make a list of responses on newsprint or markerboard. Ask:

- How complete would you regard a biography that only pays attention to its subject's birth and death? Why?
- Do you think your congregation pays too much, too little, or the right amount of attention to the events of Jesus's life other than his birth, death, and resurrection? Why?

We Believe: Leader Guide

- How much attention do you personally tend to pay to these events? Why? What single thing about the rest of Jesus's life do you find most meaningful, and why?

Distribute or display the text of the Nicene Creed. Invite participants to read it aloud, either in its entirety or from "For us and for our salvation" through "he suffered death and was buried." Read aloud from *We Believe*: In the Nicene Creed, "There is no account of [Jesus's] baptism, temptation in the wilderness, calling of disciples, transfiguration, miracles, parables, or triumphant procession into Jerusalem on Palm Sunday.... This is not to say they are unimportant, just that no one was arguing about them in Nicaea." Tell participants this session will explore some of the theological stakes in questions about Jesus's birth and death, and how the Nicene Creed answers those questions.

Opening Prayer

Gracious God, in love you gave us Jesus Christ to be the pioneer of our salvation, sharing our flesh and blood to be our merciful and faithful high priest. By your Holy Spirit, may this time of study and conversation help us hold firm to the hope we confess, trusting that you hold firm in faithfulness to us. Amen.

Watch Session Video

Watch the Session 3 video segment together. Discuss:

- Which of Michael's statements most interested, intrigued, surprised, or confused you? Why?
- What questions does this video segment raise for you?

Fully, Truly Human

In a conversational mini-lecture, share this information from *We Believe* with participants:

For Us and for Our Salvation

- The word *Docetism*, from the Greek word for "to appear" or "to seem," refers to the idea that Jesus was only divine and simply *seemed* to be human.
- Docetism had been active for more than a century by the time of the Council of Nicaea.
- The Nicene Creed rejected Docetism by stressing that Jesus became "truly human."
- Athanasius of Alexandria (circa 296–373), one of the council's younger participants, was a staunch defender of Jesus's full, true humanity, "possessing a real and not illusory body."

Discuss:

- Michael writes that, like Arianism, Docetism was a "well-meaning heresy." What problem(s) did Docetism attempt to solve? What other problems did it introduce?
- Why did the Council of Nicaea think it important to reject Docetism as a heresy?
- Do you think any Scriptures could be read as supporting the docetic view? If so, which ones? How do the whole New Testament canon and the Nicene Creed help interpret these Scriptures?
- Where and how, if at all, is Docetism still present in church and culture today?
- What are some other ways you well-meaning people try to defend God's divinity? How do you and your congregation respond?

The Word Became Flesh

Recruit a volunteer to read aloud John 1:1-5, 14 (or 1:1-18). Discuss:

- What or who is "the Word" of which John writes? How is the Word related to God?

- What does it mean to call this Word "the light of all people" (v. 4; see also v. 9) that "darkness did not overtake" (v. 5)?
- When did the Word become flesh (v. 14), and what happened as a result?
- The Word's becoming flesh in Jesus is called the Incarnation (from the Latin *carnis*, "flesh" or "meat"). The Incarnation "gives us a better, more complete view of God," writes Michael, adding that "Jesus is God fleshed out for us." What practical, specific difference does or ought the Incarnation make for Christians' ideas and language about God?

Tell participants they will now consider the Incarnation from another Gospel's perspective. Recruit three volunteers to read aloud Luke 1:26-38, taking the roles of the narrator, Gabriel, and Mary. Discuss:

- How is Luke's account of the Incarnation like and unlike John's?
- Does Jesus's conception seem like a "partnership of Mary and the Holy Spirit" to you, as it does to Michael? Why or why not?
- How does Mary's response to God's word contrast with the response of Pontius Pilate, the only other historical human beings (apart from Jesus) mentioned in the Nicene Creed? (See John 18:37-38.)
- How easily do you identify with Mary's faithfulness? Why?
- "When the chasm [between heaven and earth] seemed far too wide, and every attempt of ours to build a bridge back to God had failed, Jesus was born to start the construction from both sides." What do you think about Michael's image for the Incarnation? What other images or metaphors help you understand the Incarnation?

- How do John's and Luke's stories of the Incarnation complement each other? What might we fail to understand about the Incarnation if we did not have them both?
- What questions do you still have about the Incarnation?

A Particular Scandal

Recruit a volunteer to read aloud Luke 2:1-5. Discuss:

- Why does Luke put down "historical and geographical markers" to identify the "days" (v. 1) of Jesus's birth?
- How do the historical particulars Luke lifts up invite contrasts between the foci of the world's attention and God's attention?
- "Theologians have called the focus on particulars like this the 'scandal of particularity.'" Why does Michael say these particulars are scandalous? Do you think the world or the Church, or both, still finds God's particular, limited focus scandalous? Why or why not?
- How can and do Christians guard against the "scandal of particularity" becoming an occasion for arrogance and exclusivity?
- How does the "scandal of particularity" mirror the scandal Docetism attempted to address?
- When, if at all, has your or your congregation's faith led you to pay "scandalous" attention to particular people, places, or issues? What happened?

For Our Sake

Recruit a volunteer to read aloud Isaiah 53:4-6 (or, preferably, 52:13–53:12). Discuss:

- Why does the "servant" (52:13) in this passage suffer? What does his suffering accomplish?

- Who might Isaiah's original audience, some six centuries before Jesus, have understood this suffering servant to be?
- How did early Christians see Jesus in Isaiah's words? (See Matthew 8:14-17; Acts 8:32-35; 1 Peter 2:21-25.)
- Do the meanings Isaiah's words had in his own time and the meaning Christians later found, and still find, in those same words contradict or invalidate each other? Complement each other? Neither? Both? How so?
- How and why does the Nicene Creed connect Jesus's suffering and death with his incarnation?
- How and why does the Creed stress the reality of Jesus's death and burial?
- Michael says atonement theories attempt to answer the question of how, exactly, Jesus's death was "for our sake." Of the theories Michael mentions—penal substitutionary atonement (Jesus offers himself as a sacrifice to pay the price for our sin), *Christus victor* (Jesus is raised victorious over the powers of sin and death), and the ransom theory (Jesus takes our place and allows us to return to God)—which comes closest to your understanding of how Jesus's death is "for our sake," and why? What else do you believe about Jesus's death?
- Why do you think the Nicene Creed does not define exactly how Jesus's death is "for our sake"?
- Michael cautions, "We should be careful not to extrapolate too broadly the power of redemptive suffering." Why? How, if at all, have you encountered and responded to the belief that *all* suffering is redemptive? When, if ever, have you seen your own or another's suffering lead to some positive or even redemptive outcome?
- According to Michael, what distinction did John Wesley draw between "bearing a cross" and "taking up your cross"? Why does this distinction matter? What crosses have you

borne and what crosses have you willingly shouldered in your life?

Closing Your Session

Read aloud from *We Believe*: "Jesus was incarnate in the world for us and for our salvation, and we are called to continue that incarnating.... [Jesus] 'became flesh and blood, and moved into the neighborhood.' So...we should consider how we can move into our own neighborhoods in more real and effective ways."

Lead a discussion in which you and your participants identify specific ways in which, individually and as a congregation, you are "moving into your neighborhoods"—the areas in which you live, work, study, play, and worship—for others' sake in Jesus's name, sharing his love in truly human, embodied ways.

Closing Prayer

For your closing prayer, sing together or read this verse from "O Love, How Deep, How Broad, How High" (attr. Thomas á Kempis; trans. Benjamin Webb, 1852; https://hymnary.org/text/o_love_how_deep_how_broad_how_high), or another hymn or song you think relates to the subjects of this session.

O love, how deep, how broad, how high,
how passing thought and fantasy,
that God, the Son of God, should take
our mortal form for mortals' sake!

SESSION 4

In Accordance with the Scriptures

Session Goals

This season's reading, discussion, and prayer will help participants:

- reflect on their experience making plans as an analogy for the plans of God;
- consider how Christians have read certain Old Testament texts as anticipations of Jesus, and ponder whether and how these readings continue to be valid today;
- ponder what Luke's account of the risen Jesus's appearance to disciples on the road to Emmaus (Luke 24:13-35) means about encountering the risen Jesus today;
- explore the significance of Jesus's ascension by studying Luke's account of the event (Acts 1:6-11);
- understand the significance of the assertion that Jesus is at God's right hand; and
- reflect on the significance of Jesus's promised second coming and judgment.

Biblical Foundations

Now on that same day two of them were going to a village called Emmaus, about seven miles from Jerusalem, and talking with each other about all these things that had happened. While they were talking and discussing, Jesus himself came near and went with them, but their eyes were kept from recognizing him. And he said to them, "What are you discussing with each other while you walk along?" They stood still, looking sad. Then one of them, whose name was Cleopas, answered him, "Are you the only stranger in Jerusalem who does not know the things that have taken place there in these days?" He asked them, "What things?" They replied, "The things about Jesus of Nazareth, who was a prophet mighty in deed and word before God and all the people, and how our chief priests and leaders handed him over to be condemned to death and crucified him. But we had hoped that he was the one to redeem Israel. Yes, and besides all this, it is now the third day since these things took place. Moreover, some women of our group astounded us. They were at the tomb early this morning, and when they did not find his body there they came back and told us that they had indeed seen a vision of angels who said that he was alive. Some of those who were with us went to the tomb and found it just as the women had said, but they did not see him." Then he said to them, "Oh, how foolish you are and how slow of heart to believe all that the prophets have declared! Was it not necessary that the Messiah should suffer these things and then enter into his glory?" Then beginning with Moses and all the prophets, he interpreted to them the things about himself in all the scriptures.

Luke 24:13-27

So when [Jesus and his disciples] had come together, they asked him, "Lord, is this the time when you will restore the kingdom to Israel?" He replied, "It is not for you to know the times or periods that the Father has set by his own authority. But you will receive power when the Holy Spirit has come upon you, and you will be my witnesses in Jerusalem, in all Judea and Samaria, and to the ends of the earth." When he had said this, as they were watching, he was lifted up, and a cloud took him out of their sight. While he was going and they were gazing up toward heaven, suddenly two men in white robes stood by them. They said,

We Believe: Leader Guide

> *"Men of Galilee, why do you stand looking up toward heaven? This Jesus, who has been taken up from you into heaven, will come in the same way as you saw him go into heaven."*
>
> Acts 1:6-11

Before Your Session

- Carefully and prayerfully read this session's Biblical Foundations, more than once. Note words and phrases that attract your attention, and meditate on them. Make special note of how these Gospel stories are the same and different. Write down questions you have, and try to answer them, consulting trusted Bible commentaries.
- Carefully read chapter 4 of *We Believe*, more than once.
- You will need either Bibles for in-person participants or screen slides prepared with Scripture texts for sharing (identify the translation used), or both; newsprint or a markerboard and markers (for in-person sessions); paper, pens or pencils (in-person).
- If using the DVD or streaming video, preview the Session 4 video segment. Choose the best time in your session plan for viewing it.
- Put the text of the Nicene Creed (in the translation your denomination or congregation uses, if applicable) either on a paper handout, a slide for screen sharing, or both.

Starting Your Session

Welcome participants. Invite volunteers to talk about a time they made a plan. (You may want or need to begin discussion by talking about your own experience.) Discuss:

- Did your planning pay off? Why or why not?
- With the benefit of hindsight, would you plan differently for the same experience? Why or why not?
- What are the characteristics of a good plan?

In Accordance with the Scriptures

- Who is the best planner you've ever known? Why?
- How do you respond to someone who says, "God has a plan"?
- How might God's plans be like or unlike human plans?

Distribute or display the text of the Nicene Creed. Invite participants to read it aloud, either in its entirety or from "On the third day" through "his kingdom will have no end." Point out that this section of the Creed says Jesus's resurrection was "in accordance with the Scriptures" to affirm that Jesus's life, death, and future all were and are planned by God. The "Scriptures" here refer to the Old Testament, in which Christians have often found "hints" or "clues" of Jesus's incarnation, crucifixion, resurrection, and second coming. Read aloud from *We Believe*: "There is something hopeful and delightful knowing that all of this [i.e., salvation through Jesus] was done according to God's plan, 'in accordance with the Scriptures.'"

Opening Prayer

Immortal and eternal God, in the resurrection of your Son Jesus Christ you opened the way to eternal life for us. May the same Spirit who raised Jesus from the dead raise our spirits to your side in this time of study, that our trust in him may increase and we may grow as his ever more faithful witnesses. Amen.

[margin note: *Read aloud*]

Watch Session Video

Watch the Session 4 video segment together. Discuss:

- Which of Michael's statements most interested, intrigued, surprised, or confused you? Why?
- What questions does this video segment raise for you?

A Long Time Coming

Form four small groups of participants. Ask each small group to read and discuss one of the Scriptures cited below. Instruct each group

39

to discuss this question: "How could Christians see this Scripture anticipating Jesus"?

- Genesis 22:1-14 (read also Hebrews 11:17-19)
- Psalm 139
- Hosea 6:1-3
- Jonah 1:11–2:10 (read also Matthew 12:38-42)

After allowing time for reading and discussion, reconvene the whole group, and invite a member of each small group to briefly discuss highlights from their small group's discussion. Use some or all of these question to extend discussion:

- How is the test God sets for Abraham in Genesis 22 like and unlike what God does in Jesus?
- How did Abraham, "figuratively speaking," receive Isaac back from the dead, as the author of Hebrews teaches (11:19)?
- What language, if any, in Psalm 139 leads you think about Jesus, and why?
- How did Hosea 6:1-3 originally call ancient Israel to repentance? How, if at all, does it lead you to think about Jesus?
- How is Jonah like and unlike Jesus? How does Jesus use Jonah's story to answer the religious authorities who are opposed to him (Matthew 12:38-42)?
- How natural or forced, easy or difficult does this way of reading the Old Testament seem to you, and why? How convincing do you find these interpretations, and why?
- How, if at all, does looking for anticipations of Jesus in the Old Testament affect our understanding of what this Scripture meant to its original audience, or what it means to Jewish people today?
- Can Christians affirm the Old Testament as a witness to Jesus without perpetuating stereotypes of and prejudice

In Accordance with the Scriptures

toward Jews and Judaism today? If so, how? If not, why not?

A Predicted Surprise

Recruit volunteers to read aloud Luke 24:13-27 (28-35), taking the roles of the <u>narrator</u>, <u>Jesus</u>, and the <u>two disciples</u>. [*one person*] Discuss:

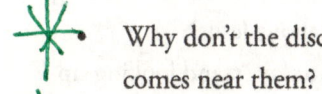

- Why don't the disciples recognize the risen Jesus when he comes near them?
- Why does Jesus ask Cleopas and the other disciple to tell him "the things about Jesus of Nazareth" (v. 19)?
- How would you evaluate the two disciples' summary of Jesus's ministry, death, and resurrection, and why? What, if anything, would you want to add? What, if anything, would you want to omit?
- Why does Jesus call the disciples "foolish" and "slow of heart to believe" (v. 25)?
- What do you think experiencing a Bible study led by Jesus would be like? What particular Scripture, if any, would you want Jesus to interpret for you?
- Why does Jesus act "as if he [is] going on" when they reach Emmaus (v. 28)?
- Why do the disciples recognize Jesus as he blesses, breaks, and gives them bread?
- How, if at all, do you believe the risen Jesus has shown himself to you or to your congregation, or both?
- What, if anything, does these disciples' experience show disciples today about meeting and recognizing Jesus?

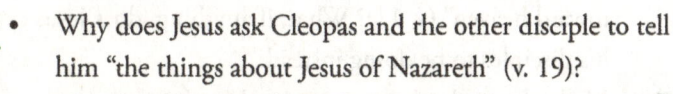

The Ascension

Recruit volunteers to read aloud Acts 1:6-11, taking the roles of the narrator, Jesus, the disciples, and the angels. Discuss:

41

We Believe: Leader Guide

- What are Jesus's disciples hoping his resurrection means? How does Jesus correct their expectations?
- What does Jesus promise his disciples? How has this promise been fulfilled?
- What is the farthest place you or your congregation have witnessed to Jesus, and how?
- Why do the angels ask the disciples what they are looking at? What do the angels tell them about Jesus?
- How, if at all, do Jesus's disciples today "stand looking up toward heaven" (v. 11)? What, if anything, does Jesus expect his disciples to be doing instead?
- Michael says the Ascension completes Jesus's "round-trip journey" from heaven to earth and back again and means "no place would be outside of his experience and presence." What practical difference does Jesus's ascension make to your faith? Why?

Seated at the Right Hand

Recruit a volunteer to read aloud Psalm 110. Discuss:

- To whom is this psalm addressed, and what promises does it make?
- What is the significance of sitting at God's "right hand" (v. 1)? Of God being at one's "right hand" (v. 5)?
- Who was Melchizedek (v. 4; see Genesis 14:17-20)? What do you think it means to be a priest like Melchizedek?
- Read Mark 12:35-37 (parallels Matthew 22:41-46; Luke 20:41-44). How and why does Jesus apply this psalm to himself?
- As Michael notes, "Psalm 110…is the New Testament's most quoted psalm." Read each of these Scriptures and explain how they apply the psalm to Jesus: Acts 2:32-35; 1 Corinthians 15:20-28; Hebrews 5:5-10 and 7:15-22.

- Read John 14:1-3. What does Jesus promise his disciples about his presence at God's side?

The Second Coming and the Judgment

Discuss:

- How much do you think about the second coming of Jesus? Does it seem more of a promise or a threat, or neither, to you? Why?
- Michael writes, "Parousia is the technical term used to describe Jesus's second coming," and refers to a visit like a king's visit. What does this image communicate and fail to communicate about Jesus's second coming?
- Read Matthew 24:36-44. What does Jesus tell his disciples about his coming again?
- How do Jesus's disciples, two thousand years later, "keep awake" in anticipation of Jesus's coming?
- "We should not fear Christ's coming and judgment," writes Michael, "but should welcome it." In your experience, do Christians mostly fear or welcome Christ's coming and judgment? Why?
- Read Ezekiel 34:17-22. How is the promise that God will judge between God's sheep good news?
- Read Malachi 3:2-3. How, if at all, does envisioning judgment as a cleansing shape your understanding of and attitude toward it?

Closing Your Session

Read aloud from *We Believe*: "Hardship can and does come our way, but our salvation is secured. Because our salvation always goes according to God's plan." Read aloud Romans 8:38-39. Encourage participants, as your group read or sings this session's Closing Prayer,

We Believe: Leader Guide

to think about some hardship they or a loved one are facing, as well as the words from Romans.

Closing Prayer

For your closing prayer, sing together or read the spiritual "He is King of Kings, He is Lord of Lords" (African American spiritual; https://hymnary.org/text/he_is_king_of_kings_he_is_lord_of_lords), or another hymn or song you think relates to the subjects of this session.

He is King of kings, he is Lord of lords,
Jesus Christ, the first and last;
no one works like him.

SESSION 5

With the Father and the Son

Session Goals

This season's reading, discussion, and prayer will help participants:

- reflect on their understanding of and attention to the Holy Spirit;
- appreciate the Nicene Creed's teaching about the Spirit;
- explore the apostle Paul's teaching about the Spirit as the source of life in Romans 8:5-17, asking how this teaching shapes Christian ethical responsibility to life;
- ask what it means to affirm that the Spirit speaks for God, as Jesus affirms in his Farewell Discourse (John 14:15-17; 16:12-15), and what the Spirit's continuing work means for disagreement in the Church today; and
- identify specific ways in which they and their congregations can follow the Spirit in activities that give life.

Biblical Foundations

For those who live according to the flesh set their minds on the things of the flesh, but those who live according to the Spirit set their minds on the things of the Spirit. To set the mind on the flesh is death, but to set the mind on the Spirit is life and peace. For this reason the mind that is set on the flesh is hostile to God; it does not submit to God's law—indeed, it cannot, and those who are in the flesh cannot please God.

But you are not in the flesh; you are in the Spirit, since the Spirit of God dwells in you. Anyone who does not have the Spirit of Christ does not belong to him. But if Christ is in you, then the body is dead because of sin, but the Spirit is life because of righteousness. If the Spirit of him who raised Jesus from the dead dwells in you, he who raised Christ Jesus from the dead will give life to your mortal bodies also through his Spirit that dwells in you.

So then, brothers and sisters, we are obligated, not to the flesh, to live according to the flesh—for if you live according to the flesh, you will die, but if by the Spirit you put to death the deeds of the body, you will live. For all who are led by the Spirit of God are children of God. For you did not receive a spirit of slavery to fall back into fear, but you received a spirit of adoption. When we cry, "Abba! Father!" it is that very Spirit bearing witness with our spirit that we are children of God, and if children, then heirs: heirs of God and joint heirs with Christ, if we in fact suffer with him so that we may also be glorified with him.

Romans 8:5-17

[Jesus said,] "If you love me, you will keep my commandments. And I will ask the Father, and he will give you another Advocate, to be with you forever. This is the Spirit of truth, whom the world cannot receive because it neither sees him nor knows him. You know him because he abides with you, and he will be in you. . . . I have said these things to you while I am still with you. But the Advocate, the Holy Spirit, whom the Father will send in my name, will teach you everything and remind you of all that I have said to you."

John 14:15-17, 25-26

[Jesus said,] "I still have many things to say to you, but you cannot bear them now. When the Spirit of truth comes, he will guide you into all the truth, for he will not speak on his own but will speak whatever he hears, and he will declare to you the things that are to come. He will glorify me because he will take what is mine and declare it to you. All that the Father has is mine. For this reason I said that he will take what is mine and declare it to you."

John 16:12-15

Before Your Session

- Carefully and prayerfully read this session's Biblical Foundations, more than once. Note words and phrases that attract your attention, and meditate on them. Make special note of how these Gospel stories are the same and different. Write down questions you have, and try to answer them, consulting trusted Bible commentaries.
- Carefully read chapter 5 of *We Believe*, more than once.
- You will need either Bibles for in-person participants or screen slides prepared with Scripture texts for sharing (identify the translation used), or both; newsprint or a markerboard and markers (for in-person sessions); paper, pens or pencils (in-person).
- If using the DVD or streaming video, preview the Session 5 video segment. Choose the best time in your session plan for viewing it.
- Put the text of the Nicene Creed (in the translation your denomination or congregation uses, if applicable) either on a paper handout, a slide for screen sharing, or both.

Starting Your Session

Welcome participants. Ask participants what they think about when they think about the Holy Spirit. Write responses on newsprint or markerboard. Discuss:

- What Scriptures about the Holy Spirit can you remember or locate?
- When and how does your congregation talk about the Holy Spirit in worship?
- Michael writes that "the Holy Spirit tends to be minimized in the eyes and hearts of some Christians." Do you agree? If not, why not? If so, what do you think accounts for this minimization?
- How important would you say the Holy Spirit is to your personal faith? Why?

Distribute and/or display the text of the Nicene Creed. Invite participants to read it aloud, either in its entirety or from "We believe in the Holy Spirit" through "who has spoken through the prophets." Tell participants this session will help them explore the Nicene Creed's teaching about the Holy Spirit.

Opening Prayer

Creator God, in the beginning your Spirit brooded over watery chaos, summoning light and life. Your Spirit breathed words of challenge and comfort for your servants, the prophets, to share with your people. Your Spirit rested on your Son, Jesus Christ, and raised him from the dead that we might live eternally. May your same Spirit move among and within us in this time of study, that in your light, we may see light, and may more fully experience and extend to others the life you give. Amen.

Watch Session Video

Watch the Session 5 video segment together. Discuss:

- Which of Michael's statements most interested, intrigued, surprised, or confused you? Why?
- What questions does this video segment raise for you?

"We Believe in the Holy Spirit"

In a conversational mini-lecture, share this information from *We Believe* with participants:

- Like many creeds predating it, the Nicene Creed adopts a trinitarian format, with sections focusing on the Father, the Son, and the Holy Spirit.
- Because theological controversies about the Father and the Son's relationship dominated the Council of Nicaea, the nature and work of the Spirit received less attention. Some later creeds, such as the Athanasian Creed, further elaborate on the Spirit.
- The Nicene Creed stresses the Spirit's equal standing with the Father and the Son—a more literal translation reads "who together with the Father and the Son are worshiped together and glorified together."
- Western, Latin-speaking Christians later inserted the phrase "and the Son" (*Filioque*), referring to from whom the Spirit proceeds, into the Nicene Creed. This "*Filioque* clause" was a cause of the Great Schism between the Western Church and the Eastern, Greek-speaking (Orthodox) Church in 1054.

Discuss:

- "It is difficult to wrap our heads around the truth that we worship one God who is yet three Persons." How do you think about the Trinity? How important is this teaching to your personal faith, and why?
- "The triune nature of God is not something we must understand before we can believe it. Rather, we believe it first, and then we experience it." When, if ever, have you experienced God as Trinity?

We Believe: Leader Guide

- "God's threefold nature, while not explicitly spelled out in Scripture, is self-evident in his creation. Everything leads to an understanding that our God is indeed three Persons." Do you agree with Michael that God's trinitarian nature is "self-evident"? Why or why not?
- Why did the Council of Nicaea reject the idea that the Holy Spirit is "more of a 'servant'" who is subordinate to the Father and Son? How does this idea contradict or threaten scriptural views of the Spirit? How, if at all, is this idea about the Spirit present in Christianity today?
- What difference does it make to claim that that the Spirit proceeds from the Father alone, or from the Father and the Son? Do you think continued disagreement between the Western and Eastern Church over the *Filioque* clause detracts from the Nicene Creed's value as a statement of basic Christian belief, or damages the cause of Christian unity? Why or why not?

Life-Giver

Recruit a volunteer to read aloud Romans 8:9-17. Discuss:

- Who is the Holy Spirit, according to Paul in this passage? What does the Spirit do? What is the Spirit's relationship to God? To Christ?
- What is the Spirit's connection to life?
- What do these Scriptures say about the Spirit's connection to life? Genesis 2:4b-7; Psalm 104:24-30; Ezekiel 37:1-6.
- What, if anything, does the Spirit's connection to life suggest about Christians' ethical responsibilities toward life?
- How is the Spirit's connection to life the same as or different than "life in the Spirit"?
- What contrasts does Paul draw between living "in the flesh" and living "in the Spirit"? How can we know whether we live according to the flesh or the Spirit?

- How does the Spirit make us God's children? What benefits or privileges do God's children have?
- How is suffering with Christ (v. 17) different from other suffering? Should Christians seek out such suffering? Why or why not? Do you believe you have ever suffered for Christ? If so, how so?

Spoken... and Speaking?

Recruit one volunteer to read aloud John 14:15-17 and another to read aloud John 16:12-15. Tell participants these verses are part of Jesus's long Farewell Discourse in John's Gospel, the teaching he gave his disciples before his arrest and crucifixion. Discuss:

- What does Jesus teach about who the Holy Spirit is and what the Spirit does?
- What does Jesus say about the relationship between the Father, Son, and Spirit?
- What does Jesus say about the relationship between the Spirit and his disciples? Between the Spirit and the world?
- How do these other Scriptures show the Spirit speaking for God? Numbers 11:24-30; Joel 2:28-31 (see also Acts 2:14-21); Isaiah 61:1-4 (see also Luke 4:16-21).
- Do you believe the Spirit still speaks for God? If so, how do we recognize such speech? If not, why not?
- Michael argues that, beyond "the unalterable essentials" of what the Nicene Creed outlines, the Church has "liberty to argue" about other beliefs and practices. What examples of these kind of disagreements have you encountered personally, if any? What can and should Christians do when they disagree with one another about such matters?
- Michael expresses confidence the Spirit will never contradict what he calls "the guardrails of the Nicene Creed." Do you share his confidence? Why or why not? Could you imagine

an "essential" the Nicene Creed does not address about which Christians could or do disagree? If so, what might it be? If not, why not?
- How can and do we ensure we are "seek[ing] the Spirit's guidance with our whole selves" in the midst of disagreements with other Christians?

Closing Your Session

Read aloud from *We Believe*: "As we remember that the Nicene Creed asserts that the Holy Spirit is 'the giver of life,' we are led to follow the Spirit into those things which give life." Summarize the way Michael's congregation raised money to pay off medical debt in their community. Lead participants in brainstorming specific ways your congregation or your study group, and you as individuals, can and will "follow the Spirit into those things that give life." As appropriate, assign particular follow-up steps to members of your group.

Closing Prayer

For your closing prayer, sing together or read the spiritual "I'm Gonna Sing When the Spirit Says Sing" (African American spiritual; https://hymnary.org/text/im_going_to_sing_when_the_spirit_says), or another hymn or song you think relates to the subjects of this session.

I'm gonna sing when the Spirit says sing,
I'm gonna sing when the Spirit says sing,
I'm gonna sing when the Spirit says sing,
and obey the Spirit of the Lord.

SESSION 6

One, Holy, Catholic, and Apostolic

Session Goals

This season's reading, discussion, and prayer will help participants:

- identify the Nicene Creed's four marks of the Church, explaining what they originally meant and appreciating their significance for the Church today;
- explore a sample of New Testament teaching (from 1 Corinthians 12; Ephesians 4, and 1 Peter 3) about the nature of the Church, with attention paid to the meaning of Christian baptism;
- understand biblical grounds for the Creed's teaching about the next life and articulate their own beliefs about the Resurrection and the world to come; and
- reflect on their engagement with the Nicene Creed during this study, and make plans for continuing their engagement with it.

Biblical Foundations

For just as the body is one and has many members, and all the members of the body, though many, are one body, so it is with Christ. For in the one Spirit we were all baptized into one body—Jews or Greeks, slaves or free—and we were all made to drink of one Spirit.

Indeed, the body does not consist of one member but of many. If the foot would say, "Because I am not a hand, I do not belong to the body," that would not make it any less a part of the body. And if the ear would say, "Because I am not an eye, I do not belong to the body," that would not make it any less a part of the body. If the whole body were an eye, where would the hearing be? If the whole body were hearing, where would the sense of smell be? But as it is, God arranged the members in the body, each one of them, as he chose.

1 Corinthians 12:12-18

I, therefore, the prisoner in the Lord, beg you to walk in a manner worthy of the calling to which you have been called, with all humility and gentleness, with patience, bearing with one another in love, making every effort to maintain the unity of the Spirit in the bond of peace: there is one body and one Spirit, just as you were called to the one hope of your calling, one Lord, one faith, one baptism, one God and Father of all, who is above all and through all and in all.

Ephesians 4:1-6

For Christ also suffered for sins once for all, the righteous for the unrighteous, in order to bring you to God. He was put to death in the flesh but made alive in the spirit, in which also he went and made a proclamation to the spirits in prison, who in former times did not obey, when God waited patiently in the days of Noah, during the building of the ark, in which a few, that is, eight lives, were saved through water. And baptism, which this prefigured, now saves you—not as a removal of dirt from the body but as an appeal to God for a good conscience, through the resurrection of Jesus Christ, who has gone into heaven and is at the right hand of God, with angels, authorities, and powers made subject to him.

1 Peter 3:18-22

One, Holy, Catholic, and Apostolic

Before Your Session

- Carefully and prayerfully read this session's Biblical Foundations, more than once. Note words and phrases that attract your attention, and meditate on them. Make special note of how these Gospel stories are the same and different. Write down questions you have, and try to answer them, consulting trusted Bible commentaries.
- Carefully read chapter 6 and the conclusion of *We Believe*, more than once.
- You will need either Bibles for in-person participants or screen slides prepared with Scripture texts for sharing (identify the translation used), or both; newsprint or a markerboard and markers (for in-person sessions); paper, pens or pencils (in-person).
- If using the DVD or streaming video, preview the Session 6 video segment. Choose the best time in your session plan for viewing it.
- Put the text of the Nicene Creed (in the translation your denomination or congregation uses, if applicable) either on a paper handout, a slide for screen sharing, or both.
- *Optional*: Obtain a copy of the baptismal liturgy (if any) your congregation uses or arrange to show a video recording of a baptism in your congregation, or both.

Starting Your Session

Welcome participants. Ask:

- What is the Church?
- What are the essential attributes or characteristics of the Church?

List participants' responses on newsprint or markerboard.

Distribute or display the text of the Nicene Creed. Invite participants to read it aloud in its entirety, since this is your study's

55

We Believe: Leader Guide

last session. Tell participants that in its final section, the Creed identifies four essential characteristics, or *marks*, of the Church, and that in this session, they will study those marks and what they mean for Christians today.

Opening Prayer

[read aloud]

Holy God, in every age you call a holy people to yourself, empowered to proclaim your will and to embody your love. May your Holy Spirit so fill us now that we may hear and heed your summons in new ways, rejoicing that you have claimed and called us to live as the body of your Son and our Savior Jesus Christ in the world today. Amen.

Watch Session Video

Watch the Session 6 video segment together. Discuss:

- Which of Michael's statements most interested, intrigued, surprised, or confused you? Why?
- What questions does this video segment raise for you?

On Your Marks

Ask participants to talk briefly about their initial reactions to the four "marks of the Church" identified in the Nicene Creed: one, holy, catholic, apostolic. Discuss each in turn, using the questions below:

One

- ✱ How many churches have you been a part of in your life? Do you think of all those churches as belonging to "one" Church? If so, how? If not, why not?
- Why does the Nicene Creed say the Church is "one"?
- As Michael notes, the word for "church" in New Testament Greek is *ekklesia*, "assembly" or "those called out." Who "calls out" the Church, and from what or from where?

One, Holy, Catholic, and Apostolic

- Jesus prayed his followers might "all be one" (John 17:21). Does the existence of many churches today undercut or negate Jesus's prayer? If so, how? If not, why not?
- Can the Church be "one" without being a single, unified institution? Why or why not?
- Does insisting that the Church is "one" obscure or minimize real and important differences between Christian traditions? Why or why not?

Holy

- How do you define holiness?
- Why does the Nicene Creed say the Church is "holy"?
- As Michael states, "holy" means "different" or "set apart by and for God." What evidence do you see to support the claim the Church is holy in this sense? What evidence against this claim do you see?
- Why does God choose a "holy people" in Scripture? (Read also Exodus 19:1-6; Matthew 5:43-48; 1 Peter 2:9-10.)
- "The command to be holy is also a promise from the God who commanded it, because [God] is the only one who can make us holy." When and how, if at all, have you seen God keep the promise of holiness to the Church?

Catholic

- As Michael states "catholic" means "universal," "worldwide," or, more literally, "according to the whole." Why does the Nicene Creed say the Church is "catholic"?
- "Because the Church is catholic," writes Michael, "any Christian anywhere is part of the Church everywhere." If such is the case, why don't all Christian churches recognize those outside their own membership as part of the Church? How should Christians respond if other Christians question their membership in the catholic Church?

- "The Church being catholic also means that every Christian can find themselves at home within each branch of the Christian family." When and how, if ever, have you found yourself "at home" in a branch of the Church other than your own?

Apostolic

- As Michael states, the root of the word *apostolic* is *apostle*, or one who is sent. Why does the Nicene Creed say the Church is "apostolic"?
- Does your tradition or denomination claim "an unbroken chain of leadership that reaches back to the original apostles"? If so, why does it believe this chain of leadership is important? If not, why not?
- Michael says the Church also understands itself as "apostolic" because "its teachings trace back to the original apostles." Who determines whether a teaching is apostolic, and how?
- How have attempts to return to apostolic faith and practice renewed the Church throughout its history? If your own tradition or denomination is the result of such a renewal, how was it an attempt to recover apostolic teaching?
- How does privileging the authority and teaching of the first apostles benefit the Church today? Does or could this emphasis ever hinder the Church? Why or why not?

One Church, One Baptism

Form three groups of participants. Instruct each group to read and discuss one of the following Scriptures, paying close attention to what it teaches about the Church:

- 1 Corinthians 12:12-18
- Ephesians 4:1-6
- 1 Peter 3:18-22

One, Holy, Catholic, and Apostolic

After allowing time for small group discussion, reconvene the whole group and invite a volunteer from each group to talk briefly about highlights from their discussion. Extend discussion with some or all of these questions:

- The image of the Church as a body appears in both 1 Corinthians 12 and Ephesians 4. How is the Church like and unlike the human body?
- How do 1 Corinthians 12 and Ephesians 4 talk about the Spirit's connection to the Church? How is the Spirit's presence in the Church both a gift and a responsibility?
- What do these three Scriptures teach about baptism in the Church? How do they align with the Nicene Creed's teaching about baptism?
- How is Christian baptism like and unlike the baptism of repentance practiced by John the Baptist?
- Who does your church baptize? Why? How does your congregation prepare people for baptism?
- Why does the Church recognize only baptisms performed in the name of the triune God?
- Michael states "the Church is God's vehicle for salvation in the world." Does your church see itself as an "ark of salvation"? Why or why not?
- "If boredom or complacency ever set in, it is likely an urging of the Spirit to set out for new, uncharted waters!" In what "new, uncharted waters" might the Spirit be urging your congregation to set sail today? What can and will you do about this call?

Optional: Before discussing baptism, review with your group the baptismal liturgy used in your congregation or watch a recording of a baptism performed in your congregation, or both.

We Believe: Leader Guide

The Resurrection and the Life

Recruit a volunteer to read aloud John 11:17-27. Discuss:

- What are your hopes, if any, about what happens after death?
- What does the Nicene Creed teach about resurrection and the world to come? What questions does it leave unanswered?
- What does Jesus mean when he calls himself "the resurrection and the life" (v. 25)?
- "Too much of religion these days treats eternity as an escape from life on earth," writes Michael. Do you agree with his assessment? Why or why not? How do you understand eternity?
- "Our life in 'the world to come' will be embodied, just as Christ rose bodily." (Read also 1 Corinthians 15:50-57.) What does the promise of an embodied resurrection tell us about the significance of bodily life? How is it like or unlike much popular thought, inside and outside the Church, about the next life?
- "In the end, God's creation is not abandoned; it is redeemed." Read Revelation 21:1-5; 22:1-5. How does Revelation envision God's redeemed creation? What do these visions of the world to come imply, if anything, about how we ought to live in and relate to the world as it currently is?

Closing Your Session

Read aloud from *We Believe*: "The words of the [Nicene] creed have an ability to burrow into our hearts and into the deepest reaches of our minds. They connect us to the living core of our faith. When combined with other things like Scripture reading, corporate worship, and prayer, the Nicene Creed breathes a life into your faith that makes it exciting and joy-filled. What's more, the Nicene Creed also holds the potential to reinvigorate your church."

Talk briefly about what you have gained most from your group's study of the Nicene Creed. Invite volunteers to talk briefly about their own experience of the study. Discuss:

- What do you now appreciate most about the Nicene Creed?
- What is one question you still have about the creed, and how will you go about answering it?
- How would you suggest your congregation begin or continue using the Nicene Creed in worship? In Christian education? In other ways?

Closing Prayer

For your closing prayer, sing or read aloud together this verse from "The Church's One Foundation" (S. J. Stone, 1866; https://hymnary.org/text/the_churchs_one_foundation); or another hymn or song you think relates to the subjects of this session.

The church's one foundation
is Jesus Christ, her Lord;
she is His new creation,
by water and the word.
From heav'n He came and sought her
to be His holy bride;
with His own blood He bought her,
and for her life He died.

Watch videos based on *We Believe: How the Nicene Creed Can Deepen Your Faith* with Michael Carpenter through Amplify Media.

Amplify Media is a multimedia platform that delivers high-quality, searchable content with an emphasis on Wesleyan perspectives for churchwide, group, or individual use on any device at any time. In a world of sometimes overwhelming choices, Amplify gives church leaders and congregants media capabilities that are contemporary, relevant, effective and, most important, affordable and sustainable.

With *Amplify Media* church leaders can:

- Provide a reliable source of Christian content through a Wesleyan lens for teaching, training, and inspiration in a customizable library
- Deliver their own preaching and worship content in a way the congregation knows and appreciates
- Build the church's capacity to innovate with engaging content and accessible technology
- Equip the congregation to better understand the Bible and its application
- Deepen discipleship beyond the church walls

AMPLIFY MEDIA

Ask your group leader or pastor about Amplify Media and sign up today at www.AmplifyMedia.com.

www.ingramcontent.com/pod-product-compliance
Lightning Source LLC
LaVergne TN
LVHW030052200325
806393LV00004B/18